WHAT A HAM!

Make Me Laugh!

WHAT A HAM!

jokes about pigs

by Rick & Ann Walton/pictures by Joan Hanson

Lerner Publications Company · Minneapolis

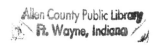
Copyright © 1989 by Lerner Publications Company

Library of Congress Cataloging-in-Publication Data

Walton, Rick.
  What a ham!

  (Make me laugh!)
  Summary: A collection of riddles about pigs, such as
"What constellation looks like a pig? The Pig Dipper."
  1. Swine—Juvenile humor. 2. Wit and humor, Juvenile.
[1. Pigs—Wit and humor. 2. Riddles] I. Walton, Ann,
1963-   . II. Hanson, Joan, ill. III. Title.
IV. Series.
PN6231.S895W35   1989   818'.5402   88-13119
ISBN 0-8225-0972-5 (lib. bdg.)

Manufactured in the United States of America

1 2 3 4 5 6 7 8 9 10 98 97 96 95 94 93 92 91 90 89

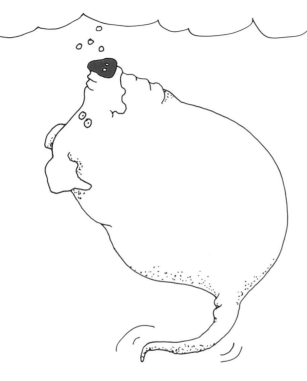

Q: What do you get when you cross a baby
   frog with a pig?
A: A pollihog.

Q: Where do you clean a dirty hog?
A: At a hogwash.

Q: Why do pigs paint themselves green?
A: So they can hide in bushes.

Q: What kind of bushes do pigs hide in?
A: Hambushes.

Q: What kind of pigs hide in hambushes?
A: Hedge-hogs.

Q: What do you get when you cross a pig with an ostrich?

A: A pig who hides her head in the mud.

Q: What's a pig's favorite pet?
A: A ham-ster.

Q: What game is played with a little white ball
that goes "b-oink, b-oink, b-oink"?
A: Pig Pong.

Q: Why isn't it much fun to play basketball with
a pig?
A: Because he's a ball hog.

Q: What do pigs put around their yards?
A: Pigget fences.

Q: What's the best way to ride a pig?
A: Piggyback, of course.

Q: Do pigs like to wear shoes?
A: No, they would rather go boar-foot.

Q: What do pigs do on Saturday afternoons?
A: Go on pignics.

Q: Who puts out fires and rolls in the mud?
A: Smokey the Boar.

Q: What does Smokey the Boar do for a living?
A: He's a Pork Ranger.

Q: What do you get when you cross a pig with a fish?

A: A boar-racuda.

Q: What kind of pig should you be careful of in a crowd?

A: A pigpocket.

Q: Where do European pigs live?

A: In Pork-tugal.

Q: Who represents the U.S. in Pork-tugal?

A: The Ham-bassador.

Q: What do you call the Pork-tuguese pigs when they move to the United States?

A: Immi-grunts.

Q: What do bald pigs wear?
A: Pig wigs.

Q: Why don't pigs have fur coats?
A: Because they can't afford to buy them.

Q: What's a pig's favorite city?
A: Piggsburgh Pen-sylvania.

Q: Where do pigs go for excitement?
A: New Pork City.

Q: Where do the pigs in New Pork City go for walks?
A: In Central Pork.

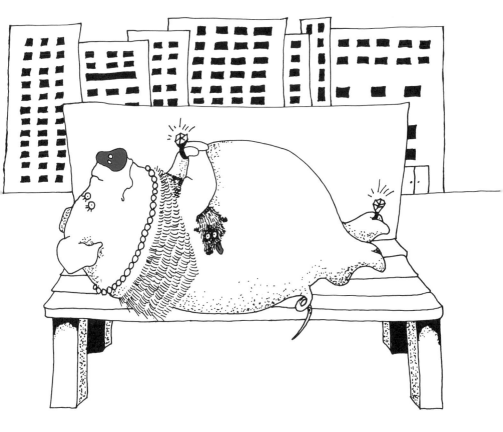

Q: Where do rich New Pork City pigs live?
A: On Pork Avenue.

Q: How much money does a pig have?
A: A pig pen-ny.

Q: How much do really dirty pigs have?
A: A scent.

Q: Where do pigs keep their money?
A: In a piggy bank.

Q: What happened when the pig got hit on the head with a rock?
A: She got ham-nesia.

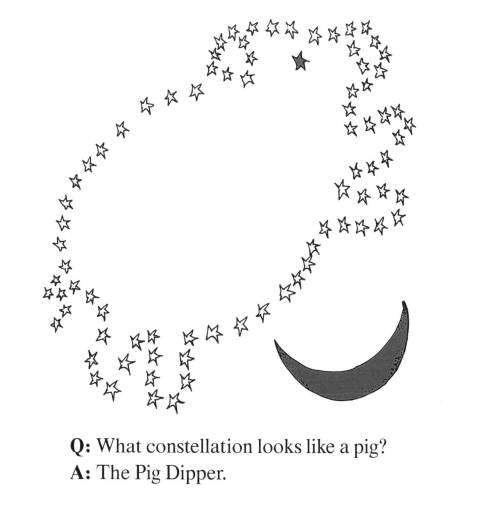

Q: What constellation looks like a pig?
A: The Pig Dipper.

Q: What sits at your door and oinks at strangers?

A: A watchpig.

Q: What does the watchpig watch out for most?

A: Ham-burglars.

Q: Where do pigs like to go to have their babies?

A: New Ham-shire.

Q: Where do momma piggies keep their baby piggies?

A: In pigpens.

Q: What do good little pigs do when they come home from school?

A: Their ham-work.

Q: Where do pigs speak Spanish?

A: In Sows America.

Q: How do you call a Chinese pig?

A: "Chop Souieec! Chop Souieee!"

Q: What did Julius Caesar's pet pig speak?

A: Pig Latin.

Q: What do you call a picture of a pig at home?
A: A pen and oink drawing.

Q: What kind of meat keeps going up and down in price?

A: See-sawsage.

Q: What do you get when you cross a pig with a skunk?

A: Bacon that stinks.

Q: Why do you seldom see pigs with glasses?

A: Because they prefer to drink out of a trough.

Q: What's green, sour, and fat?
A: A dill piggle.

Q: Why did Tom Tom the piper's son steal a pig?

A: Because he wanted to pig out.

Q: What do you know when you see three pigs wearing polka-dot shirts?

A: That you should see a doctor, quick.

Q: What do you get when you cross a pig with a giant egg?

A: Ham-pty Dumpty.

Q: What rescued Ham-pty Dumpty when he fell?

A: A ham-bulance.

Q: What musical instrument do pigs play?
A: The pigcolo.

Q: Where do pigs play their pigcolos?
A: In boarchestras.

Q: What did the scrooge pig say at Christmas?
A: Bah Ham-bug.

Q: What do you get when you mix a pig, an egg, and a cup of milk?
A: Hog nog.

Q: What do pigs use for Christmas trees?
A: Porkypines.

Q: What kind of pigs like snow?
A: Pigpen-guins.

Q: What do the Pigpen-guins live in?
A: Pigloos.

Q: Where do Pigpen-guins live?
A: At the Sows Pole.

Q: What do pigs put on their cuts?
A: Oinkment.

Q: What kind of pig saves skiers in trouble?
A: A Saint Boar-nard.

ABOUT THE AUTHORS

RICK AND ANN WALTON love to read, travel, play guitar, study foreign languages, and write for children. Rick also collects books and writes music while Ann knits and does origami. They are both graduates of Brigham Young University and live in Kearns, Utah, where Rick teaches sixth grade.

ABOUT THE ARTIST

JOAN HANSON lives with her husband and two sons in Afton, Minnesota. Her distinctive, deliberately whimsical pen-and-ink drawings have illustrated more than 30 children's books. Hanson is also an accomplished weaver. A graduate of Carleton College, Hanson enjoys tennis, skiing, sailing, reading, traveling, and walking in the woods surrounding her home.

Make Me Laugh!

CAN YOU MATCH THIS?
CAT'S OUT OF THE BAG!
CLOWNING AROUND!
DUMB CLUCKS!
ELEPHANTS NEVER FORGET!
FACE THE MUSIC!
FOSSIL FOLLIES!
GO HOG WILD!
GOING BUGGY!
GRIN AND BEAR IT!

HAIL TO THE CHIEF!
IN THE DOGHOUSE!
KISS A FROG!
LET'S CELEBRATE!
OUT TO LUNCH!
OUT TO PASTURE!
SNAKES ALIVE!
SOMETHING'S FISHY!
SPACE OUT!
STICK OUT YOUR TONGUE!
WHAT A HAM!
WHAT'S YOUR NAME?
WHAT'S YOUR NAME, AGAIN?
101 ANIMAL JOKES
101 FAMILY JOKES
101 KNOCK-KNOCK JOKES
101 MONSTER JOKES
101 SCHOOL JOKES
101 SPORTS JOKES